USBORNE

THE GREAT
HISTORY
SEARCH

Kamini Khanduri
Illustrated by David Hancock

Designed by Ian Cleaver
History consultant: Dr. Anne Millard
Series editor: Felicity Brooks

In the town on pages 34 and 35, some poor people lived in a workhouse.

On the American prairies on pages 36 and 37, many people rode in wagons.

Electric stoves were on sale in the department store on pages 38 and 39.

Turn to pages 32 and 33 to see all the people at the French ball in their best clothes.

You'll find this painting of a Dutch family on pages 30 and 31.

The Indian emperor on pages 28 and 29 sat on this beautiful throne.

The palace gardens were lit by paper lanterns at the Chinese party on pages 26 and 27.

Contents

The Incas on pages 24 and 25 played all kinds of musical instruments.

Jesters lived in medieval castles. See who else lived there on pages 22 and 23.

There was a dancing bear at the village fair on pages 20 and 21.

About this book

Early people painted pictures on their cave walls. See how they lived on pages 4 and 5.

In this book, you can find out about lots of different people and places from history. But this isn't just a history book, it's a puzzle book, too. This shows you how the puzzles work and gives you a few tips to help you solve them.

The farmers on pages 6 and 7 used tools like this sickle.

This strip tells you the date. BC is before Christ and AD is after Christ.

Around the outside of each big picture, there are lots of little pictures.

The writing next to each little picture tells you how many of that thing you can find in the big picture.

This wagon in the distance counts.

1870-1880

Prairie homes

For many years, the plains, or prairies, of North America were home to Native Americans. Then, settlers from the East took over the land, and built towns and railways. In this town, people are preparing for a holiday.

People wrote on clay tablets in the Mesopotamian city on pages 8 and 9.

Find out how the Egyptians built pyramids on pages 10 and 11.

Part of this wall has been taken away, so you can see inside.

This part of a gun counts as one gun.

This cowboy coming out of the big picture counts as a little picture too.

Instead of spotting this printing press, you have to find where it is used.

The Assyrians used siege engines in the battle on pages 12 and 13.

The puzzle is to find the people, objects and animals in each big picture. Some are easy to spot, but some are tiny, or hidden behind other things. If the big picture is in two halves (pages 4–5 and 12–13), you have to look in both halves. You'll find all the answers on pages 40–45.

Find out what the Vikings hung on their walls on pages 18 and 19.

Turn to pages 16 and 17 to find out why Romans took a flask of oil to the bath house.

People at the Greek market on pages 14 and 15 paid with coins like this one.

Early people

The old people told the children exciting stories. Can you find two storytellers?

Fish caught from the river were hung to dry on wooden frames. Spot 20.

Axes were stones on wooden handles. Find two.

People used these digging sticks to dig for roots in the ground. Spot three.

Baskets were woven from rushes. Find nine.

People made tools from flints. Spot four other people chipping away at flints.

People shot animals with bows and arrows. Spot a boy who has shot a bird.

Early people moved around with the seasons, hunting animals and gathering plants to eat. The left-hand page shows some early people in Europe, spending the winter in a cave. The right-hand page shows them in summer.

People painted animal pictures on the cave walls. Spot three deer pictures.

Lamps were made by burning fur soaked in animal fat. Find five.

Women gathered berries in leather bags. Find three bags.

4

Men went hunting for wild animals. Find seven wild deer.

Skins and furs were sewn into coverings and clothes. Find five people sewing.

Babies were wrapped up warmly. Spot nine.

People scraped skins to clean them. Spot four skins being scraped.

Paint was made from soft rocks and animal fat. Find three people making paint.

People hung skins to dry on wooden racks. Spot five.

Antler

Some tools were made from antlers. Can you find four people carving antlers?

Necklaces were made from shells, stones, bones or teeth. Find 12.

People wore furs in winter and skins in summer. Spot a child being dressed.

Wooden spears with sharp flint tips were used for hunting. Spot 11.

Meat was roasted over a fire. Spot six people cooking.

5

First farmers

Flat loaves of bread were baked on clay ovens. Can you spot eight ovens?

Wooden ladders were used for building. Find three.

Women fetched water from the stream. Find seven women with water pots on their heads.

Spot three cooking pots.

Fish were caught in the stream. Spot four people fishing with nets.

People rolled out pieces of clay to make pots. Find two people making pots.

At harvest time, crops were cut down with tools called sickles. Spot five sickles.

Farming began when people learned to plant seeds and grow crops. They also tamed animals. These changes meant people could stay in one place instead of moving around. This is a farming village in the Middle East.

Men went hunting for wild animals. Spot two men coming back from a hunting trip.

Women made thread by spinning wool around a spindle. Spot three spindles.

The chief offered gifts to a statue of the village goddess. Find the statue.

Thatched roofs on houses caught fire easily. Find a fire on a roof.

The grain from the crop was put into big baskets. Spot seven baskets.

Find two men mending the mud-brick wall around the village.

Thread was woven into cloth on a wooden frame called a loom. Spot three.

Sheep were kept for wool, milk and meat. Find 20.

Goats were kept for milk, skins and meat. Find four.

Pigs were kept for meat. Find six pigs and six piglets.

Cattle were kept for milk, skins and meat. Find 16.

Geese were kept for feathers, eggs and meat. Can you spot 11?

Children helped look after herds of animals. Find four herders with sticks.

Stones were used to grind grain into flour. Spot four women grinding.

Dogs helped with hunting and herding other animals. Spot eight.

Children scared birds away from the crops. Find four children scaring birds.

7

Most people couldn't read or write, so they hired scribes. Spot one scribe.

Wheels were made from three pieces of wood joined together. Can you spot ten?

Soldiers wore long cloaks and helmets, and carried spears. Find 16.

Baskets were used for fruit, vegetables and grain. Spot 14.

People used metal tubes as drinking straws. Spot four people using straws.

Living in cities

Furniture was made of wood. Spot five chairs.

Early cities had temples, schools and lots of houses. This city is in Mesopotamia. The temple is on a big stepped platform, called a ziggurat. People are going there in a procession, to offer gifts to the city's god.

Buildings had flat roofs. Spot 40 people on rooftops.

Merchants used donkeys to carry packs. Spot four with packs.

Rich boys went to school. Schools were very strict. Spot a schoolboy sneaking in late.

Find four people playing harps like this one.

Spot two pairs of men playing this game.

Dresses were fastened at the shoulder. Find nine women in blue dresses.

People wrote on clay tablets. Spot someone running with a message on a tablet.

Find three metalsmiths who are pouring hot metal into hollow clay shapes.

The king ruled the city. Can you see him in his chariot with the queen?

Potters made clay pots on a wheel. Spot four potter's wheels.

Jars were used to carry wine. Find someone who has broken a jar.

People used seals to sign things. The picture on the seal was rolled into soft clay. Spot one seal.

Stone seal

Rolling the seal

Picture on clay

Can you see a farmer bringing some sheep as a payment to the king?

Pyramids

The king and some other rich people kept pets. Find five dogs.

Grit

Spot four people polishing blocks with stone tools and grit.

Polishing tool

The architect planned the building. Can you see him looking at his plans?

Here's the doctor's tool basket. Find the doctor.

The queen had a pet monkey. Spot the monkey being naughty.

A ramp of rubble was built to reach the upper levels. Spot someone falling off the ramp.

Ancient Egyptian kings and queens were buried inside big stone pyramids, which were built while they were still alive. There were no machines, so a pyramid took about 20 years to build. This one is in its early stages.

This is what the finished pyramid looked like. Find two models of finished pyramids.

Mallet

Chisel

Stonemasons used chisels to chip off rough edges. Can you find six?

The king came to check on the work. Can you see him being carried in his chair?

10

Find eight men using wooden poles to lever stone blocks into place.

Teams of men pulled the blocks along on sleds. Find nine sleds.

Carpenters used hammers to mend broken sleds. Spot six hammers.

Measuring instruments were used to check each block was level. Find five.

The queen would have her own pyramid beside the king's. Spot the queen.

Oil was used to help the sleds move smoothly. Spot four jars of oil.

The overseer was in charge of the building work. Can you see him pointing angrily with his stick?

Baskets were used for carrying rubble. Find a man with a hole in his basket.

Birds called hawks looked for food around the building site. Find seven.

Metalsmiths made and mended tools. Spot three saws like this one.

Scribes made lists of how many blocks and tools were being used. Spot six scribes.

Battering ram

Going into battle

Some soldiers attacked with swords. Find 15 swords.

Siege engines with battering rams inside were used to break through the city walls. Spot five siege engines.

Can you find four horses swimming across the river?

Archers attacked with bows and arrows. Spot 12 bows.

Soldiers wore tunics, leggings and boots. Spot four soldiers putting on their boots.

Spot five soldiers carrying sacks full of stolen goods.

The Assyrian people had a big army of soldiers. The top part of this picture shows the soldiers marching into battle.

The bottom part shows them attacking a city. They stole things and captured people from the places they attacked.

Many people were captured by the soldiers. Spot seven captives with their hands tied.

Some horses wore bright saddle cloths. Spot four yellow cloths.

There was fighting on top of the walls. Spot seven people falling.

12

The soldiers stole animals. Spot seven sheep being led away.

Even children were captured. Find a mother comforting a child with a drink.

The soldiers carried shields. Spot someone who has dropped his shield.

Inflated skins were used as floats to cross rivers. Spot someone who has let go of his float.

The king rode into battle in his chariot. Can you see him?

Soldiers used ladders made of wood. Can you find eight?

Many soldiers attacked with spears. Spot a broken spear.

Slingers attacked by hurling big stones from leather slings. Can you spot seven others?

Small boats were used to carry things across rivers. Spot four boats.

Scribes made lists of how many people had been killed or captured. Find two scribes.

Soldiers on horseback were called the cavalry. Spot two soldiers on white horses.

13

At the market

The barber cut people's hair. Find a man who hates his new haircut.

This coin is from Athens. Other cities had their own coins. Spot a man dropping all his money.

Officials checked the weight of things. Find six sets of weighing scales.

People ate olives and used olive oil for cooking and in lamps. Spot someone eating olives.

Can you find four dogs?

Rich people shopped with their slaves. Spot a slave with too much shopping.

This picture shows a busy marketplace in the city of Athens in Greece. A Greek marketplace was called an agora. All the shops were under a covered area called a stoa. Out in the open, there were lots of stalls.

Soldiers had spears and big bronze helmets. Can you see five soldiers?

Cats were rare pets for rich people. Find four cats which have escaped.

Fish was a very popular food. Spot four people who have been to a fish stall.

14

Find three children playing with hoops.

 The wine-seller let some people taste his wine. Spot four people drinking wine.

 Can you find three people carrying the sandals they have bought?

 Wise men called philosophers met to discuss science and politics. Spot two arguing.

 There were often statues of gods or famous people. Find two statues.

 Lamps were the only lighting used in houses. Find the lamp stall.

People from outside the city had to change money at the banker's stall. Spot the banker.

 Rich people bought slaves. Spot a slave who is trying to escape from his new master.

 Some people wore hats when it was sunny. Find five hats.

Pottery was often beautifully painted. Spot five two-handled jars like this.

Actors in plays wore masks like this. Find three actors going to a rehearsal.

15

The bath house

To relax, people had their bodies massaged by a slave. Spot four people having a massage.

Lots of exercises went on at the baths. Find five people lifting weights.

Spot someone stealing another man's clothes from a changing room locker.

The hot room was called the caldarium. Can you find it?

The Romans made lots of statues. Can you find a statue of the emperor?

People used sticks called strigils to scrape oil and dirt off their bodies. Spot five.

Roman towns had public bath houses, with hot, warm and cold baths. People went to bathe, but also to talk about business, to exercise, or just to gossip. A visit might last hours, and lots of people went every day.

Fighting men called gladiators were very popular. Spot this gladiator with all his fans.

Women went to a separate bath house. Find five women with their towels.

People wore sandals in the hot room, so as not to burn their feet. Spot a man who has forgotten his sandals.

Apartments near the baths were noisy. Find a man who is complaining about the noise.

Instead of soap, people used oil to clean their bodies. Spot 11 oil flasks.

Find eight soldiers with their helmets.

Some floors were covered with mosaics (pictures made from pieces of stone). Spot a mosaic floor.

Attendants worked at the baths. Find an attendant with a pile of towels.

Food, such as pastries and olives, was on sale. Spot two trays of food.

The cold room was called the frigidarium. Can you see where it is?

Can you see someone putting on a toga — a very big piece of material?

People paid to enter the baths. Spot a thief who has run off with someone's purse.

Most large bath houses had a library, with scrolls to read. Find the library.

Scroll

Water was heated by a boiler over a fire. Spot a slave who has fainted from the heat.

Boiler

17

Winter feasts

Cloth was woven on a big loom. Can you see the loom?

Women fastened their tunics with brooches. Find someone doing up her brooch.

Firewood was kept outside. Spot two people gathering wood.

There were spoons and knives, but no forks. Find 12 spoons.

Women wore dresses with tunics on top. Spot someone with a torn tunic.

A poet called a skald played the harp and recited poems. Find the poet.

The Vikings lived in northern Europe. The men were fierce warriors who sailed abroad in their big ships. At home, most Vikings lived in long houses, in small villages. Here, a village chief is giving a feast in his house.

The chief had his own chair. Can you find him?

Wool tapestries hung on the walls. Find a child hiding behind one.

People sat on stools or on wooden platforms along the walls. Spot someone falling off a stool.

When they were not being used, weapons were often hung on the walls. Find five swords.

Beer, wine and mead (a honey drink) were poured from jugs. Spot six.

Acrobats entertained the guests. Find a pair of acrobats.

Food was cooked over an open fire. Spot someone stirring a cauldron full of stew.

The chief had his own servants. Spot a servant with a pile of bowls.

Oil lamps in tall metal holders lit the house. Find five.

People drank from animal horns or wooden cups. Spot 12 drinking horns.

Vegetables and dried fish were hung from the rafters. Spot ten dried fish.

Wine, beer and salted food were stored in wooden barrels. Spot seven.

Men kept hunting dogs. Can you see two fighting?

Clothes and valuable things were kept in chests. Find an open chest.

Village life

Merchants came to the fair from nearby towns. Spot a merchant unloading wine from a cart.

Hoe

Houses had vegetable plots. Spot someone using each of these tools.

Rake

Spade

Things for sale at the fair were put on tables. Spot four.

There was lots to see at the fair. Find a dancing bear.

Stocks

People who did wrong were punished. Spot a man with his legs in the stocks.

Can you see someone using stepping stones to cross the stream?

In the Middle Ages, most of the people in Europe lived in small villages. A few villagers owned their own land. The rest lived and worked on land owned by a lord. In this English village, the summer fair is being set up.

The lord lived in a big house or a castle. Can you see him setting off on a hunting trip?

People went to church often. Spot the priest sweeping the church porch.

People wore different kinds of hats. Spot ten pointed hoods.

The blacksmith made and mended metal tools. Can you find him?

Can you see three people chopping firewood outside their houses?

Milk was made into butter in a churn. Spot two churns.

Everyone had their grain ground into flour at the village windmill. Can you see it?

People kept bees for honey. Spot a man being chased by a swarm of bees.

Chickens were kept for meat, feathers and eggs. Spot two people feeding chickens.

Find the miller taking money for grinding some grain.

Can you spot someone going around selling small things from a tray?

ots of things vere bought nd sold at the air. Spot a big ile of cheeses.

Cats were useful for catching rats and mice. Find nine other cats.

Most people had fleas and head lice. Find a woman picking lice from her child's hair.

21

The jester's job was to make people laugh. Spot the jester.

Spot 20 guards on the battlements, looking out for enemies.

The waste from toilets dropped down to the ground below. Can you find two toilets?

Prisoners were kept in the dungeon. Spot a prisoner in chains.

Servants were always busy. Spot a servant with a tray of goblets.

There was enough food stored to last months. Spot the storeroom.

1300–1400

Castle life

In the Middle Ages, kings and lords in Europe built huge stone castles. Armies of fierce soldiers guarded them. The

strong, stone walls kept enemies out, but castles were often cold, damp places to live in.

The lord and his wife slept in a big bed with curtains all around it. Find the bed.

This is the lord. Can you see him in his office counting out his money?

Fierce birds called falcons were trained to hunt. Find three.

People didn't wash often. Spot someone in a bathtub.

Knights on horseback trained to fight with long spears called lances. Find four.

Tapestries helped keep out the cold. Spot someone hanging a tapestry.

Musicians called minstrels played from a gallery. Can you see them?

The castle had stone spiral staircases. Spot someone falling down the stairs.

Windows had shutters on the inside. Spot someone looking out of a window.

Find ten archers at shooting practice with their bows and arrows.

Water was pulled up in buckets from a well. Spot the well.

Find three horses looking out of their stables.

Guards who were off duty rested in the guardroom. Find the guardroom.

Everyone had a job to do. Can you see the candle-maker?

The priest held religious services in the chapel. Can you find it?

23

Inca homes

Buildings were made from stone blocks which fitted together perfectly. Spot four storehouses.

Guinea pigs were not pets, but were kept for meat. Can you find 12?

The Incas lived in the Andes mountains of South America. They built cities and strong stone roads. In this farming village, people are growing crops of corn and potatoes on terraces (steps of land dug into the mountainside).

The soft wool from alpacas was used to make clothes. Find eight.

Bridges were made out of reeds. Spot two.

Women often carried babies on their backs. Find eight babies.

Knotted strings, called quipus, were used to store information. Spot four.

Llamas were used to carry packs. Find a llama sitting down.

Messengers called chasquis ran quickly to deliver messages. Spot four.

Trumpets called pototos were made from shells. The sound carried far. Find one.

Looms had a strap, which went around the weaver's back. Spot three.

Sandal soles were made of llama skin. Find someone putting on some sandals.

This big mountain bird is a condor. Spot another one.

Spot someone making a drink called chicha by spitting chewed fruit into water.

Potatoes grew well on the high slopes. Find ten sacks of potatoes.

Wooden sticks like this were used for digging. Find ten digging sticks.

Women made flour by grinding corn between stones. Spot a woman grinding.

Cooking pots were all shapes and sizes. Find one like this.

Children scared birds away from the crops by firing stones from slings. Find two slings.

Musical instruments were played on special occasions. Spot each of these.

Panpipes

Drum

Flute

The Inca emperor was a strict ruler. Can you see him in his litter, coming to inspect the village?

Litter

A Chinese party

People used fans to keep cool. Spot three fans.

Pottery, clothes and furniture were often decorated with dragon pictures. Find eight.

Silk covers were draped over chairs. Find four chair covers.

People ate rice with almost every meal. Find a half-finished bowl of rice.

Incense burner

People burned incense to make a sweet smell. Spot an incense burner.

Many people kept pet dogs. Find seven.

Chinese emperors and noblemen lived in beautiful palaces with lovely gardens. Most other people in China were poor. In this picture, a rich nobleman is having a firework party. He is sitting on the veranda with his wife.

Wood was often covered with a shiny substance called lacquer. Find seven lacquered trays.

Find the palace gardener and his children watching the fireworks.

Gong

Drum

Flute

Musicians entertained the guests. Spot these musical instruments.

26

Men and women wore silk robes. Find eight red robes.

Fireworks were invented in China. Spot a servant lighting a firework.

Paintings on silk or paper scrolls were hung on walls. Find two.

Officials took notes at important events. Find an official with his boy assistant.

Rich people had statues in their gardens. Find two statues like this.

People poured tea from teapots and drank it from little bowls. Spot four teapots.

Lanterns were made of paper and had candles inside. Spot ten.

People used chopsticks to eat their food. Spot six pairs of chopsticks.

People went to temples but they also had shrines at home for worship. Find one.

Shrine

A type of pottery called porcelain was invented in China. Spot six jars like this one.

Screens were used as doors, or for decoration. They were often painted. Find one.

27

Indian wedding

Some people rode on elephants, on seats called howdahs. Find five elephants.

The holy man blessed the bride and groom. Can you see him?

Weavers made beautiful things from material. Find these things.

Red and gold wall hanging

Black and white cushion

Blue and green carpet

The palace had lovely gardens. Can you spot a gardener with a spade?

Can you see someone wearing this jewel in his turban?

The Mogul emperors in India were very rich. They lived in grand palaces like this one. Here, everyone is celebrating because the emperor's son is getting married. They are watching the wedding procession.

The emperor's golden throne was decorated with diamonds and rubies. Find it.

People wore gowns called jamas and trousers called piajamas. Spot a man in these clothes.

Yellow jama

Striped piajamas

Men wore turbans on their heads. Spot ten dark blue turbans.

Silver bowl

Emerald necklace

Wood and ivory box

Jade wine cup

Mogul craftsmen made lots of beautiful things. Find each of these.

The palace artist painted pictures of important events. Can you find him?

The Moguls had many weapons. Spot a dagger with a horse's head on it.

People smoked pipes called hookahs. Find a man smoking.

Spot the musicians playing these instruments.

Brass trumpet

Drum

Sitar

Tambourine

The bride and groom would not have met before the wedding. Find them.

Groom

Bride

The emperor kept birds at the palace. Find six peacocks.

Most people in India were very poor. Spot this group of beggars outside the palace.

Busy ports

Spices, such as ginger and pepper, came from the East Indies. Spot three sacks of spices.

Sailors used astrolabes on voyages, to measure the height of stars. Can you see one?

There were lots of jobs to be done, even in port. Find these workers.

Rope-fitter

Sail mender

Carpenter

Most houses were tall and narrow, with a top part called a gable. Spot a green gable.

Goods were pulled up to storerooms in attics by machines called winches. Find three.

In the 1600s, Holland was a very rich country. Big ships, owned by merchants, sailed abroad to buy and sell goods. This is a busy Dutch port. A big ship has just arrived home from a long voyage and is being unloaded.

On long voyages, fresh food ran out, so many sailors became ill or died. Spot a sick sailor.

As well as roads, many Dutch towns had canals. Find an open bridge over a canal.

Tulips were rare and expensive. Can you see some?

Artists painted pictures of merchants and their families. Spot an artist.

Ships had guns in case they were attacked by enemies. Find four guns.

The ship owner paid the crew after each voyage. Find him.

Many houses had stone fruit garlands, called swags, under their windows. Find six swags.

Sailors were often injured on voyages. Spot a sailor who has a wooden leg.

People played musical instruments at home. Find this virginal.

Rich people had servants. Spot the servants who are doing these jobs.

Hanging up laundry

Scrubbing floor tiles

Polishing silver

The telescope was invented in Holland. Spot a scientist using his telescope.

Many goods, such as tea and sugar, came from China, India or Africa. Find these things.

Porcelain

Silk

Ivory

Some rich people ran homes for orphans. Find two ladies collecting a homeless child.

At the ball

There were lots of clocks at the palace. Find two.

Men wore wigs made of goat, horse or human hair. Can you see someone whose wig has fallen off?

Both men and women made up their faces. Spot someone checking his face in a pocket mirror.

Shoes often had fine embroidery and buckles. Find these shoes.

Musicians played dance music. Can you find a harpsichord?

Women curtsied and men bowed to the King. Spot the King.

Jar of smelling salts

The French King Louis XV lived in a fine palace at Versailles, near Paris. He entertained lots of rich people there. In this picture, everyone is at a ball, in a beautiful long room called the Hall of Mirrors.

Women often fainted from the heat. Spot a maid bringing smelling salts to revive her mistress.

The Hall of Mirrors had 17 arched mirrors. Find five of them.

Most people knew the steps for many different dances. Spot a dancer who has fallen over.

The King had hundreds of servants. Can you spot a servant pouring wine?

Dresses had very wide skirts. Find eight pink dresses with this pattern.

Men wore jackets, short trousers called breeches, and silk stockings. Spot a man in these clothes.

Women wore decorations in their hair. Find 11 wearing flowers in their hair.

Women stuck beauty spots on their faces. Find four women with beauty spots.

Hanging glass holders called chandeliers held candles. Can you find four others?

The palace was full of beautiful, expensive furniture. Can you see a couch?

Oranges

Salmon

Chicken

All kinds of tasty food was served at the ball. Spot these dishes.

People drank from crystal glasses. Can you spot someone spilling her wine?

Women carried pretty, painted fans. Find 11 women peeping over their fans.

There were rules about how to behave in front of the King. Spot someone who has misbehaved.

Factory town

Children worked in mines, factories or on the streets. Spot a child selling matches.

Tray of matches

Richer people used carriages called hansom cabs as taxis. Find two.

Boats called barges were used to transport heavy goods on canals. Spot three.

People fetched water from pumps in the street. Spot someone pumping water.

Spot the people selling these things from carts or barrows.

Milk

Coal

Fruit and vegetables

This is a town in England. When big machines for making cloth and other things were invented, many country people moved to towns like this, to work in factories. The streets were noisy, crowded and dirty.

Homeless children and old people were sent to a harsh place called a workhouse. Can you find one?

Steam trains carried passengers and goods all over the country at low cost. Spot a train.

Coal was the main fuel, so lots of people worked down coal mines. Spot six miners with lamps.

Miner's lamp

Sweep's brush

Chimney sweeps climbed up dark, sooty chimneys. Spot three sweeps.

Barber's

Shoemaker's

Tailor's

People bought things from small shops. Find these shops.

Streets were lit by gas lamps. Can you spot ten?

In factories, people worked long hours. Can you spot a tired worker who has fallen asleep?

Newspapers were on sale for people who could read. Spot a paper-seller.

The police tried to stop people from causing trouble or committing crimes. Spot six policemen.

Spot the people doing these jobs on the streets.

Selling pies

Lighting lamps

Selling flowers

Some orphans lived on the streets, stealing money or begging. Spot these beggars.

The filthy streets and houses were full of rats. Spot the rat-catcher doing his rounds.

The barrel organ player entertained people in the street. Can you see him?

Barrel organ

35

Prairie homes

The blacksmith made horseshoes. Can you find him?

The sheriff had to keep law and order. He wore a star-shaped badge. Find him.

People who lived outside town came in to buy things. Spot someone buying this lamp.

There was only one school in town, with one teacher. Find the teacher.

Most people went to church on Sundays. Can you see the church?

There were no phones, but people sent messages by telegraph. Spot six telegraph poles.

For many years, the plains, or prairies, of North America were home to Native Americans. Then, settlers from the East took over the land, and built towns and railways. In this town, people are preparing for a holiday.

Some people kept on moving West. Spot a family loading their wagon.

The doctor treated people for illnesses or injuries. Can you see him?

Trains carried people, goods and cattle to other towns and cities. Find where the train stops.

Sometimes, robbers tried to steal money from the bank. Spot two.

Most men had guns. Can you find eight guns?

Handgun

Rifle

Men drank and played cards in a bar called a saloon. Spot the barman.

Wagons were used to carry heavy loads. Spot three with covers and three without.

People entertained each other with music. Find these instruments.

Accordion

Piano

Guitar

Some Native Americans lived near the town in areas called reservations. Spot four.

Many people worked on the railways. Spot five men laying new tracks.

Cowboys brought cattle into town. Spot eight other cowboys.

Richer people owned small carriages called buggies. Can you find two?

The local newspaper was printed once a week. Spot the newspaper office.

Printing press

37

Department stores

When the first department stores opened, people could buy all kinds of things in one building, instead of going to lots of shops.

Spot a fashion show going on in the women's clothes department.

All kinds of toys were sold in the toy department. Spot six of each of these.

Teddy bear

Grey rocking horse

Red pedal car

Can you see where people are buying baby clothes?

Paperback books didn't cost much. Spot someone buying this book.

People played records on a phonograph. Spot someone choosing one.

The store had its own letter box where mail was collected. Find it.

Jars of orange bonbons

Chocolates on stands

Tins of toffees

Spot these things in the confectionery department.

The store had a hairdressing salon. Spot three people having their hair cut.

Milkshakes were sold at a soda fountain. Can you see it?

Electric heaters warmed houses quickly. Spot six like this.

Radios called wirelesses were a new invention. Find three like this.

The glass and china department was full of fragile things. Spot someone who has broken a vase.

People could now buy many useful electrical goods. Spot three of each of these.

Washing machine

Vacuum cleaner

Stove

The store sold shoes for adults and children. Find two people trying on shoes.

Can you spot four attendants wearing uniforms like this?

There were phones in the store for people to use. Spot two.

Boxes of cereal

Strings of sausages

Bottles of tomato ketchup

Food was sold in the grocery department. Can you find these groceries?

39

Early people 4–5

Storytellers 1 2
Fish 3 4 5 6 7 8 9
    10 11 12 13 14 15
    16 17 18 19 20
    21 22
Axes 23 24
Digging sticks 25
    26 27
Baskets 28 29 30
    31 32 33 34
    35 36
People chipping
away at flints 37 38
    39 40 41
Deer pictures 42 43
    44
Lamps 45 46 47 48
    49
Leather bags 50 51
    52
Child being dressed
    53
Spears 54 55 56 57
    58 59 60 61 62
    63 64
People cooking 65
    66 67 68 69 70

Necklaces 71 72 73
    74 75 76 77 78
    79 80 81 82
People carving
antlers 83 84 85 86
Wooden racks 87
    88 89 90 91
People making paint
    92 93 94
Skins being scraped
    95 96 97 98
Babies 99 100 101
    102 103 104
    105 106 107
People sewing 108
    109 110 111 112
Wild deer 113
    114 115 116 117
    118 119
Boy who has shot a
bird 120

First farmers 6–7

Ovens 1 2 3 4 5
    6 7 8
Ladders 9 10 11
Women with water
pots 12 13 14 15 16
    17 18
Cooking pots 19
    20 21
People fishing 22
    23 24 25
People making pots
    26 27
Men returning from
hunt 28 29
Spindles 30 31 32
Statue 33
Herders 34 35 36
    37
Women grinding 38
    39 40 41
Dogs 42 43 44 45
    46 47 48 49
Children scaring
birds 50 51 52 53
Geese 54 55 56 57
    58 59 60 61 62
    63 64

Cattle 65 66 67 68
    69 70 71 72 73
    74 75 76 77 78
    79 80
Pigs 81 82 83 84
    85 86
Piglets 87 88 89 90
    91 92
Goats 93 94 95 96
Sheep 97 98 99
    100 101 102 103
    104 105 106 107
    108 109 110 111
    112 113 114 115
    116
Looms 117 118 119
Men mending wall
    120 121
Baskets 122 123
    124 125 126 127
    128
Roof on fire 129
Sickles 130 131 132
    133 134

Living in cities 8–9

Scribe 1
Wheels 2 3 4 5 6 7
    8 9 10 11
Soldiers 12 13 14 15
    16 17 18 19 20
    21 22 23 24 25
    26 27
Baskets 28 29 30
    31 32 33 34 35
    36 37 38 39 40
    41
People using straws
    42 43 44 45
People on roofs 46
    47 48 49 50 51
    52 53 54 55 56
    57 58 59 60 61
    62 63 64 65 66
    67 68 69 70 71
    72 73 74 75 76
    77 78 79 80 81
    82 83 84 85
Donkeys with packs
    86 87 88 89
Late boy 90
Stone seal 91
Farmer with sheep
    92

Person who has
broken jar 93
Potter's wheels 94
    95 96 97
King 98
Metalsmiths 99 100
    101
Messenger 102
Women in blue
dresses 103 104
    105 106 107 108
    109 110 111
Pairs of men playing
game 112 113
People playing harps
    114 115 116 117
Chairs 118 119 120
    121 122

Pyramids 10–11

Dogs 1 2 3 4 5
People polishing 6 7
 8 9
Architect 10
Doctor 11
Monkey 12
Pyramid models 13
 14
Chisels 15 16 17 18
 19 20
King 21
Hawks 22 23 24 25
 26 27 28
Saws 29 30 31
Scribes 32 33 34
 35 36 37
Man with hole in
basket 38
Overseer 39
Oil jars 40 41 42
 43
Queen 44
Measuring
instruments 45 46
 47 48 49
Hammers 50 51 52
 53 54 55
Sleds 56 57 58 59
 60 61 62 63 64

Men using poles 65
 66 67 68 69 70
 71 72
Person falling off
ramp 73

Going into battle 12–13

Siege engines 1 2 3
 4 5
Swimming horses 6
 7 8 9
Bows 10 11 12 13
 14 15 16 17 18 19
 20 21
Soldiers putting on
boots 22 23 24 25
Soldiers with sacks
 26 27 28 29 30
Captives 31 32 33
 34 35 36 37
Yellow cloths 38 39
 40 41
People falling 42 43
 44 45 46 47 48
Boats 49 50 51 52
Scribes 53 54
Soldiers on white
horses 55 56
Slings 57 58 59 60
 61 62 63 64
Broken spear 65
Ladders 66 67 68
 69 70 71 72 73
King 74
Person who has let
go of float 75

Person who has
dropped shield 76
Mother giving drink
to child 77
Sheep 78 79 80 81
 82 83 84
Swords 85 86 87
 88 89 90 91 92
 93 94 95 96 97
 98 99

At the market 14–15

Man dropping his
money 1
Weighing scales 2 3
 4 5 6 7
Person eating olives
 8
Dogs 9 10 11 12
Slave carrying too
much shopping 13
Soldiers 14 15 16 17
 18
Cats 19 20 21 22
People who have
been to fish stall 23
 24 25 26
Hats 27 28 29 30
 31
Two-handled jars 32
 33 34 35 36
Actors 37 38 39
Escaping slave 40
Banker 41
Lamp stall 42
Statues 43 44
Philosophers 45 46
People carrying
sandals 47 48 49
People drinking wine
 50 51 52 53

Children playing with
hoops 54 55 56
Man who hates his
haircut 57

The bath house 16–17

People having a massage 1 2 3 4
People lifting weights 5 6 7 8 9
Person stealing clothes 10
Caldarium 11
Statue 12
Gladiator 13
Women 14 15 16 17 18
Man who has forgotten sandals 19
Thief 20
Library 21
Slave who has fainted 22
Person putting on toga 23
Frigidarium 24
Food trays 25 26
Attendant with towels 27
Mosaic floor 28
Soldiers 29 30 31 32 33 34 35 36
Oil flasks 37 38 39 40 41 42 43 44 45 46 47

Complaining man 48
Strigils 49 50 51 52 53

Winter feasts 18–19

Person doing up brooch 1
People fetching wood 2 3
Spoons 4 5 6 7 8 9 10 11 12 13 14 15
Person with torn tunic 16
Poet 17
Chief 18
Child hiding behind tapestry 19
Person falling off stool 20
Barrels 21 22 23 24 25 26 27
Fighting dogs 28 29
Open chest 30
Dried fish 31 32 33 34 35 36 37 38 39 40
Drinking horns 41 42 43 44 45 46 47 48 49 50 51 52
Lamps 53 54 55 56 57
Servant with pile of bowls 58

Person stirring cauldron 59
Pair of acrobats 60
Jugs 61 62 63 64 65 66
Swords 67 68 69 70 71
Loom 72

Village life 20–21

Merchant unloading wine 1
Person using hoe 2
Person using rake 3
Person using spade 4
Tables 5 6 7 8
Dancing bear 9
Person in stocks 10
Lord 11
Priest 12
Pointed hoods 13 14 15 16 17 18 19 20 21 22
Cheeses 23
Cats 24 25 26 27 28 29 30 31 32 33
Woman picking lice from hair 34
Person selling things from a tray 35
Miller 36
People feeding chickens 37 38
Man being chased by bees 39
Windmill 40
Churns 41 42

People chopping wood 43 44 45
Blacksmith 46
Person using stepping stones 47

Castle life 22–23

Bed 1
Lord counting money 2
Falcons 3 4 5
Person in a bathtub 6
Horses looking out of stables 7 8 9
Guardroom 10
Candlemaker 11
Chapel 12
Well 13
Archers 14 15 16 17 18 19 20 21 22 23
Person looking out of window 24
Person falling down stairs 25
Group of minstrels 26
Person hanging a tapestry 27
Knights on horseback 28 29 30 31
Storeroom 32
Servant with tray of goblets 33

Prisoner in chains 34
Toilets 35 36
Jester 37
Guards on battlements 38 39 40 41 42 43 44 45 46 47 48 49 50 51 52 53 54 55 56 57

Inca homes 24–25

Storehouses 1 2 3 4
Alpacas 5 6 7 8 9 10 11 12
Bridges 13 14
Babies 15 16 17 18 19 20 21 22
Quipus 23 24 25 26
Llama sitting down 27
Chasquis 28 29 30 31
Pototo 32
Slings 33 34
Panpipes 35
Drum 36
Flute 37
Emperor 38
Cooking pot 39
Woman grinding 40
Digging sticks 41 42 43 44 45 46 47 48 49 50
Sacks of potatoes 51 52 53 54 55 56 57 58 59 60
Person making chicha drink 61
Condors 62 63

Person putting on sandals 64
Looms 65 66 67
Guinea pigs 68 69 70 71 72 73 74 75 76 77 78 79

A Chinese party 26–27

Dragon pictures 1 2 3 4 5 6 7 8
Chair covers 9 10 11 12
Half-finished bowl of rice 13
Incense burner 14
Dogs 15 16 17 18 19 20 21
Lacquered trays 22 23 24 25 26 27 28
Gardener and his children 29
Drum 30
Gong 31
Flute 32
Shrine 33
Jars 34 35 36 37 38 39
Screen 40
Pairs of chopsticks 41 42 43 44 45 46
Lanterns 47 48 49 50 51 52 53 54 55 56
Teapots 57 58 59 60

Statues 61 62
Official with boy assistant 63
Paintings 64 65
Servant lighting a firework 66
Red robes 67 68 69 70 71 72 73 74
Fans 75 76 77

Indian wedding 28–29

Elephants 1 2 3 4 5
Holy man 6
Red and gold wall hanging 7
Black and white cushion 8
Blue and green carpet 9
Gardener with spade 10
Throne 11
Man in yellow jama and striped piajamas 12
Dark blue turbans 13 14 15 16 17 18 19 20 21 22
Bride 23
Groom 24
Peacocks 25 26 27 28 29 30
Group of beggars 31
Musician playing sitar 32
Musician playing tambourine 33
Musician playing drum 34

Musician playing brass trumpet 35
Man smoking 36
Dagger with horse's head 37
Palace artist 38
Jade wine cup 39
Silver bowl 40
Emerald necklace 41
Wood and ivory box 42
Person wearing turban jewel 43

Busy ports 30–31

Astrolabe 1
Rope-fitter 2
Sail mender 3
Carpenter 4
Green gable 5
Winches 6 7 8
Sick sailor 9
Open bridge 10
Tulips 11
Scientist using telescope 12
Ivory 13
Silk 14
Porcelain 15
Ladies collecting orphan 16
Servant polishing silver 17
Servant scrubbing floor tiles 18
Servant hanging up laundry 19
Virginal 20
Sailor with wooden leg 21
Swags 22 23 24 25 26 27
Ship owner 28
Guns 29 30 31 32

Artist 33
Sacks of spices 34 35 36

At the ball 32–33

Person whose wig has fallen off 1
Person checking his face in a pocket mirror 2
Embroidered pink shoes 3
Harpsichord 4
King 5
Maid bringing smelling salts to her mistress 6
Arched mirrors 7 8 9 10 11
Dancer who has fallen over 12
Person spilling wine 13
Women peeping over fans 14 15 16 17 18 19 20 21 22 23 24
Person who has misbehaved 25
Chicken 26
Salmon 27
Oranges 28
Couch 29

Chandeliers 30 31 32 33 34
Women with beauty spots 35 36 37 38
Women wearing flowers in their hair 39 40 41 42 43 44 45 46 47 48 49
Man in blue jacket and green breeches 50
Pink dresses 51 52 53 54 55 56 57 58
Servant pouring wine 59
Clocks 60 61

Factory town 34–35

Hansom cabs 1 2
Barges 3 4 5
Person pumping
water 6
Person selling coal 7
Person selling fruit
and vegetables 8
Person selling milk 9
Workhouse 10
Train 11
Miners 12 13 14 15
16 17
Beggars 18
Rat-catcher 19
Barrel organ player
20
Person selling
flowers 21
Person lighting lamps
22
Person selling pies
23
Policemen 24 25 26
27 28 29
Paper-seller 30
Sleeping factory
worker 31

Gas lamps 32 33
34 35 36 37 38
39 40 41
Tailor's 42
Barber's 43
Shoemaker's 44
Chimney sweeps 45
46 47
Child selling matches
48

Prairie homes 36–37

Sheriff 1
Person buying lamp
2
Teacher 3
Church 4
Telegraph poles 5 6
7 8 9 10
Family loading their
wagon 11
Doctor 12
Place where train
stops 13
Cowboys 14 15 16
17 18 19 20 21
22
Buggies 23 24
Newspaper office
25
Men laying new
tracks 26 27 28 29
30
Native Americans
31 32 33 34
Guitar 35
Piano 36
Accordion 37

Wagons with covers
38 39 40
Wagons without
covers 41 42 43
Barman 44
Guns 45 46 47 48
49 50 51 52
Robbers 53 54
Blacksmith 55

Department stores 38–39

Person choosing
phonograph 1
Letter box 2
Jar of orange
bonbons 3
Chocolates on
stands 4
Tins of toffees 5
Attendants 6 7 8 9
Phones 10 11
Boxes of cereal 12
Strings of sausages
13
Bottles of tomato
ketchup 14
People trying on
shoes 15 16
Washing machines
17 18 19
Stoves 20 21 22
Vacuum cleaners 23
24 25
Person who has
broken a vase 26
Brown square
wirelesses 27 28 29
Pink electric heaters
30 31 32 33 34
35

Soda fountain 36
People having their
hair cut 37 38 39
Place where people
are buying baby
clothes 40
Red pedal cars 41
42 43 44 45 46
Grey rocking horses
47 48 49 50 51
52
Teddy bears 53 54
55 56 57 58
Fashion show 59
Person buying
orange book 60

What are they doing?

You can find each of these people somewhere in the little pictures earlier in this book. To do this puzzle, you'll need to look back and find where they come from.

1. Which of these people is painting a picture?

A   B   C   D   E   F

2. Which of these children is late for school?

A   B   C   D   E   F

3. Which of these people is going into battle?

A   B   C   D   E   F   G

4. Which of these women is a queen?

A   B   C   D   E   F   G

5. Which of these people is telling a story?

A   B   C   D   E   F

6. Which of these pairs of people is in the middle of an argument?

A   B   C   D   E

The answers are on page 48

Index

Answers to the puzzle on page 46: 1C 2F 3A 4F 5B 6D

Cover designed by Hannah Ahmed • Additional editing by Ben Denne • Proofreading by Claire Masset

With thanks to:
Mr Fred Redding, Company Archivist, Selfridges, London • The Archive Departments at Harrods Ltd
and John Lewis Partnership • Rachael Swann for checking puzzles